P9-BZB-442

Snow Angels

SNOW ANGELS by Lynn Valentine

Published by PREMIUM PRESS AMERICA

Copyright © 2001 by Lynn Valentine

All rights reserved. No part of this book may be reproduced or transmitted in any form or by any means, electronic or mechanical, including photocopying, recording, or by any information storage and retrieval system, without prior written permission of the Publisher, except where permitted by law.

ISBN 1-887654-61-5

Library of Congress Catalog Card Number applied for

PREMIUM PRESS AMERICA gift books are available at special discounts for premiums, sales promotions, fund-raising, or educational use. For details contact the Publisher at P.O. Box 159015, Nashville, TN 37215, or phone toll free (800) 891-7323 or (615)256-8484, or fax us at (615)256-8624.

For more information visit our web site at *www.premiumpress.com.*

Editor: Elizabeth B. Schnitzer
Cover and Interior Design by Bob Bubnis/BookSetters
First Edition 2001
1 2 3 4 5 6 7 8 9 10

Snow Angels

MORE

MIRACLES AND MESSAGES

LYNN VALENTINE

PREMIUM PRESS AMERICA
NASHVILLE, TENNESSEE

Table of Contents

Introduction

Behold, I send an Angel before thee,
to keep thee in the way,
and to bring thee into the place
which I have prepared.

—Exodus 23:20

This verse is about going on a journey. It comes from the book of Exodus which details the journey of God's chosen people from bondage in Egypt toward freedom in the promised land. Since writing my first book *Angels Everywhere*, I too, have been on a journey, and in the process I have learned more about myself, more about others, and more about God.

What I learned is that no matter what happens in life, God never leaves or forsakes you. He is right there in the middle of it, waiting to share as much of your burden as you are willing to let go of. Like a father watching over a toddler, he sometimes stands just out of reach —ready to catch and steady us, if we start to fall.

In this book, you will find stories detailing God's continuing intervention in the lives of ordinary people. Some are dramatic, and supernatural as angels come to the rescue, and others are about the way God uses people to do the work of angels. In either case, they show that God is involved in life and that He cares about what happens.

My prayer is that after reading this book, you will look for God's footprints in the snow around you, and realize that He is active in your life too. I also pray that you will begin to look for ways to become the "angel" that God uses to bless others. Who knows, maybe your story will be the next one we tell.

Blessings,
Lynn Valentine

Dedication

To my husband, my love, my one.

Forever and a day.

Yours.

an·gel n. An immortal being attendant upon God; a very kind and lovable person; a helping or guiding spirit.

Acknowledgments

I would like to thank God for giving me this job in His plan. I truly love my work, and I am blessed when I hear how people have been touched by the stories in these books.

I also wish to thank the contributors who have so willingly shared their experiences with me so that I can pass them on to you.

I would like to thank my wonderful agent, Bruce Barbour, and George and Bette Schnitzer, who are not only my publishers, but also my friends.

Special thanks to Patsy for always encouraging me and reminding me that I am doing God's work.

A tear-filled thank you to my best friend Andie, for standing by me, behind me, and in front of me, every time I needed her.

I also want to thank my kids for waiting on mommy as she made another book. I love you.

THE ANGEL OF THE

LORD ENCAMPETH

ROUND ABOUT THEM

THAT FEAR HIM, AND

DELIVERETH THEM.

—PSALM 34:7

Yes, I Believe

&

I am a 59 year-old woman and have been a Christian for most of that time. All my life I have believed in guardian angels, and wanted to meet mine very badly. On November 30th, 2000, I finally did.

A dear friend of mine is a bell-ringer for the Salvation Army. One day he had some errands that he just couldn't put off and asked me if I would ring the bell for him for a couple of hours. As it was the holidays it seemed like the perfect gift to give him, so I agreed.

When I got there, I noticed that he would say "Merry Christmas" to the people who gave a donation, so when I took over, I thought I would add my own touch and say, "Thank you—may God bless you—Merry Christmas".

I was actually having a good time with it until about halfway through my shift when some tough looking boys came along. They looked to be in their late teens, standing at a distance—watching as one person after another put money in the bucket. I normally wouldn't judge someone by their appearance, but there was a mean look in their eyes as they watched the bucket and whispered among themselves.

I became afraid.

Tension filled the air. They seemed like they were just waiting for a break in the crowd—watching for the moment they could make their move. My heart began to pound harder as the last of a group of people made their way past me.

Once they were gone, there would be no more witnesses. I would be alone.

I looked to my right and left, hoping to see someone coming. Nobody was around.

Then, as I turned to see where the gang of boys were, out of nowhere, standing beside me was a beautiful young man. He was dressed in black slacks and a jacket. I noticed he was wearing a lot of gold jewelry around his neck and bracelets on both wrists. What really caught my eye was a lime green cloth bracelet with white writing on it. I was so hoping it was a *What Would Jesus Do?* bracelet, but all I could see was the word, "YES". There was more written there but I couldn't make it out.

His presence kept the boys at bay for the time being, so I felt a wash of relief. He sat down on a bench only a few feet from me and began to watch as a few more people came by and placed money in the bucket. For a minute the way he watched the bucket made me wonder if he was a thief too.

Almost as fast as the thought crossed my mind he got up and put $2.00 in the bucket.

"Thank you," I said. "May God bless you and have a Merry Christmas." He only nodded.

All the while the boys remained standing there—still plotting. The tall young man then turned to face them. Quietly, and without a word, he looked each one of them directly in the eyes. In seconds their expressions went from tough to terrified, and they took off, almost running.

The young man once again took his seat on the bench.

As grateful as I was to be saved from the gang, there was something scary and odd about the young man too. From the time he had first walked up, he had not once looked at me and he never smiled. Instead he had this stern, serious expression as he kept looking past me into the parking lot. I began to feel fear well up again.

Almost as if he could read my mind, he turned to me for the first time and said, "You're tired, aren't you?"

"Yes, I worked all day before coming here and my old back is killing me." Like a soldier minding his post he continued to keep watch.

My eyes caught a glimpse of the green bracelet again. For some reason I can't explain, I had this desperate desire to see what was on it.

Before I could get a look at his arm, I noticed my friend had returned from his errands. As I was watching my friend walk towards me, the young man got up from the bench, turned to me, and said, "I've noticed something about you. Every time someone drops money in the bucket, you say 'God bless you'. Do you really mean it?"

I said, "Yes, from the bottom of my heart."

He remained completely expressionless.

I asked him for the time and as he turned his arm I could finally see what was on the bracelet. The words read, "Yes, I believe."

A sense of peace and relief washed over me. Just then he smiled at me and said, "You're safe now, you don't have to be afraid anymore."

He began to walk away, passing my friend as he came up to relieve me. In an instant, he was gone.

Later that night my friend and I talked about my experience and the young man who saved me. He said that he had seen nobody with me. . . that I was alone.

"You *had* to have seen him, he walked right between us!"

"Brenda, I didn't see anyone on the bench or anywhere near you. I only saw you."

Right then I knew that while my friend didn't see him, I was not alone and will never be alone again.

—*Brenda Collins*

Sold Out for Days

A dear friend of mine named Karen is the mother of five children consisting of toddler quadruplets and a delightful three-year old named Amanda.

Amanda had been a good girl all year and all she wanted for Christmas was "Barney Banjo." When we found out that her mom wasn't able to buy one, some friends of mine from Bible Study and I decided to try our luck.

This toy was really hard to find. As it happens every Christmas, there is always one toy that is impossible to get, and this was Barney's year. However, a local department store flyer was advertising them, so we took a chance and headed out for the store.

When we got there I made my way through the crowd, looking up and down the aisles at picked over shelves. It wasn't long however, before I realized that the toy I was after, was gone.

Discouraged, we began to head out, when this clerk came around the corner holding a Barney Banjo. Without saying a word she held it out for me to take.

I said thank you, but she remained silent. As I took it from her, I noticed that her name tag said "Karen". I grinned at the thought of it—a clerk named Karen helping us help our friend Karen.

I went up to the register to purchase the toy and all the employees looked at us in disbelief, asking us where we found Barney Banjo. They said the store had been sold out of them for days. Then things became very mysterious. When I told them that the clerk in the back named Karen found it for us, none of them knew who I was talking about. Nobody by that name even worked there.

When we returned home, I called our friend Karen and told her that Amanda was going to get her toy after all. She was so happy I could almost feel her smile through the phone. When I told her about the clerk that shared her name she started to cry.

I think she was an angel sent to answer a mother's prayer.

—Mark Hoffman

. . . in every thing by prayer and supplication with thanksgiving let your requests be made known unto God.

Phillipians 4:6

REPUTATION IS WHAT

MEN AND WOMEN

THINK OF US;

CHARACTER IS WHAT

GOD AND ANGELS

KNOW OF US.

—THOMAS PAINE

God's Timing

*T*hree years ago on Christmas Day my father was kicked in the head by one of our horses. We found him laying in the barn unconscious.

At the hospital we were told by the chief of neurology that he had a fractured skull and severe brain damage. The doctors told my family and I that there was no possible chance my dad would survive with trauma this serious. An EEG showed that his brain was swelling so badly that he would eventually die.

After the third day they told us that the only way he would remain alive was if they removed the back part of the brain. To do this would leave him in a vegetative state the rest of his life. Dad was always very active, and we knew that he wouldn't want to live that way.

The doctors said that it was impossible for him to survive without the operation—we would need a miracle.

We prayed for that miracle, but despite our prayers and pleading, they pronounced him dead on the fourth day.

All the machines that were keeping him alive were shut off... and they took him away. We all sobbed, knowing that our prayers failed.

Then, within ten minutes, the doctors came running, pushing Dad's bed back into the room. His heart was beating again! The doctors looked as white as ghosts and couldn't understand how he came back to life.

We were all so happy. Despite this miracle, the doctors remained skeptical, saying that even though he came back, he would still be brain damaged. They warned that at best he wouldn't even be 50% of who he was if he survived.

We thanked God though and put our faith in Him. After all, God proved the the doctors wrong before.

Three months later, my Dad came home and we celebrated Christmas. To this day, Dad is alive and 100% of the person he used to be. He is back to work, and is back to training and riding the horses that he and I love so much.

My father should have never survived that accident, but he did. All those prayers went out, and a Christmas miracle happened. Now I never doubt the Lord... he saved my father and my family.

—Amber Jacoby

I LOOKED AT GOD

AND HE LOOKED AT ME,

AND WE WERE

ONE FOREVER.

—CHARLES H. SPURGEON

The Test

۶

It was around the holidays—in the dead of winter when Bob and I decided to drive to Florida. He was a boat enthusiast at the time and there was some big boat racing event that he really wanted to see. So, we packed up our motor home and headed east.

We went through sleet, snow and generally very cold weather on the way to the races, but as we got closer to the southeast corner of the state, the snow turned to rain. While passing through a particularly small town, it started coming down really hard. We were barely able to see even with the windshield wipers at full swing, and more than a little hungry, so we decided to stop somewhere and eat.

We found a cute little coffee shop along the street and with no other food prospects in sight, decided to give their menu a try. Thankfully, we had an umbrella or we would have been soaked to the skin in seconds.

We enjoyed a great dinner. It felt good to be in the warmth of the coffee house.

We waited awhile for the storm to subside, but when it looked like no end was in sight we got our umbrella to brave the elements. As we left the coffee house, we were suddenly surprised to see a man appear right next to us. He looked to be middle aged, with a contagious smile. The odd thing about him was that his clothes were as dry as a bone. Even the brim of his hat, which surely would have caught some rain in this deluge, was dry.

I cannot remember his exact words after this many years but he asked if we could show him some charity. Without much thought, Bob took out his wallet and gave this man some bills. The man smiled and said we would be blessed.

We went on our way and the man went toward the coffee house door. As Bob and I walked down the steps, I remarked about how his clothes were dry. Bob noticed it too. We looked back and the man was gone.

Curiosity got the best of us, so we turned and went back into the restaurant. He wasn't there. We even went back outside and looked up and down the vacant streets, but he was nowhere to be found. There was no place for him to go. He simply disappeared.

We call him the Florida Angel, and have told many about this experience. Whenever it rains, I think of him, and am reminded of that verse in the Bible that warns us to be careful when we entertain strangers, because we may be entertaining angels unaware.

—Patsy and Bob Weikart

If any man's work comes through the test,
he will have a reward.
1 Corinthians 3:14

An angel's figure

carved in snow

is heaven's gift to

those who know

like the shape of

wings above

God's arms are open

and filled with love.

—ANDIE DAWN

Angel on the Phone

❧

$\mathcal{I}$ was experiencing the roughest time in my life. I had been suffering from anorexia, my three year old baby girl had come down with Bells Palsy, and my mother had been diagnosed with Parkinson's Disease. Other family problems were beginning to mount too, pushing me to a point where I just couldn't take it anymore. At 32 years old, I had a breakdown.

During this time, I was given medication, and scheduled therapy, but nothing seemed to work. Medication was a band-aid for the internal wounds that wouldn't heal, and therapy was nothing more than a man in a chair writing in notebooks.

It was just before Christmas—the time of the year when everyone is supposed to be happy, but I was at the end of my rope and ready to give up.

It was then that I got the strangest phone call.

It was a woman, who called me by name and told me that if I called this radio station within thirty minutes, I would win a thousand dollars. At first I was skeptical, but the woman persisted. I asked her for her name and her phone number but she wouldn't give it and hung up the phone.

Needing the money enough to chance looking like a fool if the lady was wrong, I looked up the station's number and called it. Sure enough, I had won the money!

After the excitement, I thought of this woman, wishing I could call her and thank her. I suddenly remembered that I had caller ID, so I checked it, only to see the word, "error" on the screen. My caller ID never said that before.

In a few minutes, the phone rang again and it was the woman! She asked if I won, and I said "yes!" I offered her some money, but she refused in a calm and friendly voice.

Then, she began to tell me how sad the tone of my voice was. I was far from sad, I won a thousand bucks, but she heard something under my excitement that I didn't know was there. She began to tell me that I was self-destructing.

How did she know? I wondered as she then began telling me about myself, and my problems.

I was beginning to get scared when she asked me if I knew what quicksand was. When I said that I did, she said that I was sinking in it, and she was going to throw me a rope.

She told me that in 48 hours help would come, and that I was to heed it.

I asked her how she knew all of this, and who she was and why she was doing this, but she refused to answer.

After she hung up, I checked my caller ID again, hoping it worked this time, but just as it did before, it said "error". I called the operator asking her to check who the caller was, but they had no record of a telephone call at that time.

The next day I took the dog to the groomer, and she said "Karen, you look terrible!" I said "thank you" and laughed.

"You're so thin and frail and pale. Are you okay?" she asked.

"Not really," I confessed. I explained about my breakdown and after patiently listening, she wrote down a title of a book and handed it to me.

"I don't read books!" I replied.

"READ IT!" she insisted.

I thought of what the caller told me about finding help within 48 hours, and how I was to heed it, so I took the paper, and bought the book.

The book did help me see things differently, and in time, I was eating again, feeling more like myself. I changed how I reacted to things, how I allowed others to treat me, and my outlook on life itself.

Those mystery phone calls not only gave me money for my Christmas shopping that year, but they also gave me my spirit back.

Who was the caller? How did she know what I was going through? Why did the caller ID come up "error" and how did she know this book would help me when nothing else did?

I truly believe this was an angel who called me that day.

—*Karen J*

Whomever turns someone from the error of their ways, will save them from death....
James 5:20

As the flower

turns to the sun,

or the dog to his

master, so the soul

turns to God.

—William Temple

GIVE YOUR LIFE TO

GOD; HE CAN DO

MORE WITH IT

THAN YOU CAN!

—DWIGHT L. MOODY

Roadside Angel

It was Christmas Eve and I was driving home on a dark, rural highway when I came upon a wreck. A car was burning in the middle of the road and I was apparently the first one on the scene of a collision that happened only moments before.

As I jumped out of my car I could see a man lying on his back exactly in the center of the road. I ran up and checked for a pulse, but there was nothing. He had been thrown through his windshield and killed instantly.

The second car in the accident was partially blocking the road and had swung around sideways next to the burning vehicle. Inside, two badly injured teenage girls were trapped—pinned between their seat and the dashboard. There was no light except the flames from the other car and the beams from my headlights. I tried to get to the girls but the doors were both jammed shut. I was relieved to see the girls were conscious. They began praying and screaming for help as the flames moved closer.

After a couple of minutes, another car came along and stopped. Together, the driver and I managed to smash out a window to reach the two trapped girls. We could talk to them and reach inside, but we could not get them free from beneath the dash.

A truck driver stopped and tried to put out the fire in the other car, but his small fire extinguisher soon ran out. More cars stopped and more people came running to try to help, but it just seemed hopeless.

The flames from the second car were getting hotter by the second and even tire irons and wrenches refused to budge the sealed car doors. Nothing we could do was helping and it seemed clear that within moments we were going to be driven back by the heat and flames and that the trapped girls were going to burn to death.

Suddenly a huge black man stepped out of the darkness from a field at the side of the road. I mean this guy was BIG, maybe six foot six, with a massive neck and a shaved head that glistened in the firelight. Despite the fact that it was near freezing and threatening to snow, he was barefoot and dressed only in a pair of faded bib overalls.

At the sight of the big stranger, everyone in the crowd sort of fell silent and stood back for a moment. Then, without saying a word, this huge guy just walked up to the wrecked car and literally ripped the driver's side door off of its frame with his bare hands. A couple of people rushed in and within moments we had the two injured girls away from the car. In the process of getting them out, we discovered their unconscious parents on the floor in the back seat, where they had been hurled by the force of the collision. They too, were rescued.

Within seconds of getting everyone out of the wreck, the burning car's gas tank exploded and both vehicles were fully engulfed in flames. A fire truck and ambulance arrived from a nearby town along with the local sheriff's deputy.

About then I looked around for the big barefoot hero who had saved four lives, but he was nowhere to be found. I assumed he had come from a nearby farmhouse, drawn by the flames and excitement, but the deputy taking the report informed me that there wasn't a house of any kind within two miles of the spot where the accident occurred. He also claimed that he knew everyone in the sparsely populated area and would certainly be aware of anyone who fit the description of the huge bald-headed man that I had seen.

Who was the stranger who stepped out of the darkness on Christmas Eve? I never found out, even though I was curious enough to drive back to the area a few days later and ask around at the little country market where everyone came for groceries. They had heard the story and were as baffled as everyone else. "He must have been an angel," said the little lady behind the counter. I think she was probably right.

—Michael O'Rourke

But the angel of the Lord by night opened the prison doors, and brought them forth...
Acts 5:19

WHEN YOU

CANNOT STAND,

HE WILL BEAR YOU

IN HIS ARMS.

—SAINT FRANCIS DE SALES

In an Angels Arms

֍

Christmas of 1999 was the year we finally took a vacation. We were all so excited getting to go on that "road trip" we had always promised we would take, thinking this would be a perfect time to go visit relatives we hadn't seen in quite awhile.

We left early in the morning, and the snow on the ground was nothing our brand new motor home couldn't handle. Driving along, we were singing Christmas carols and playing silly road games.

One of the games we played was where we guessed the makes and models of cars as we passed them. My husband seemed much better at this than the children or I were. My strategy was to just guess the ones I could get close to, hoping that I could spot an emblem or read something on the car that would help me score the point.

Concentrating as hard as I could, I was staring inside cars, looking for clues as I tried to win this game. That's when I saw a beat up old Buick. I recognized the car because my father had owned one when I was a baby and I had seen many pictures of it.

As I looked at the faces of the people inside, I realized that their heater was broken and they were all very cold. They were bundled up snuggly, yet shivering behind breath-fogged windows. I could see the children in the back were half asleep and quivering. Their grandfather had his arms around them trying hard to keep them warm. With our heater on, I had practically forgotten that it was winter outside, but seeing this family was a painful reminder of just how bad many people have it.

We watched them for quite a few miles. I told my husband what was going on in the car beside us and said we should do something for them. He agreed but wondered like I did about just what we could do.

Finally, they hit their turn signal to get off of the highway, so I suggested we do the same thing. I really didn't think the beat up old Buick could make it much further.

We pulled in after them at a truck stop along the road and decided we'd grab a bite to eat. After pumping their gas, the family came in from the cold, sat down at a nearby table, and ordered hot chocolates.

I watched them for awhile, and noticed that the grandfather wasn't with them. I was worried that maybe he had been forgotten in the cold car. Deciding to investigate, I walked over to the restroom, and looked out the window to where the old Buick was parked, but didn't see him.

Finally, a family in a new pickup truck with a camper shell pulled up and came inside. The two families squealed as they saw each other. They were all kissing and hugging and went out to pile into the camper. I asked my husband go and remind them of the Grandpa in the back seat of the Buick.

They looked at us as if we were nuts. They said that nobody but the kids were in the back of the car.

It was then, I realized, there was a guardian angel in the back seat keeping those little children safe and warm.

—Paula Fergueson

Then were there brought unto him little children,
that he should put his hands on them, and pray:
Matthew 19:13

It's not how much

we give but how

much love we put

into giving.

—Mother Teresa

$\mathcal{AA}$
(Angels Anonymous)

ﾟ

One Christmas some years ago, our family experienced something of a miracle.

We were very poor. My mom was trying hard, but with three kids to raise, she was fighting a losing battle. This year had been particularly bad in that we not only didn't have presents, we didn't even have food or winter coats.

Depressed, she went to an Alcoholics Anonymous meeting and told everyone there how she felt. She told them how hard it was for her to stay strong, and how she felt she was at the end of her rope. All she wanted was their prayers and to get all of this off of her chest.

When the meeting was over, a man came up to her and gave her a hug. He told her that everything would be okay, and that the main thing was for her to never quit praying, and never lose faith. He then took her hand in his. She could feel some paper squeezed between their palms. Knowing it had to be a little money, she thanked him.

When he left, she opened her hand to find $300. It was Just enough to get food, presents, and coats for Christmas. She looked everywhere for that man but he was gone. She asked everyone who was in the building, but none of them saw him hug her, or even saw him at the meeting.

She has never seen him again, but not only did he save Christmas, he saved my Mom's life. His kindness renewed her hope, strengthened her faith, and had an impact on all of our lives. So never lose hope, God always hears prayers, and in His time, He answers them too.

—Anonymous

Then you will call upon Me and go and pray to Me, and I will listen to you.

Jeremiah 29:12

We go to the grave

of a friend saying,

"A man is dead";

but angels throng

about him, saying,

"A man is born."

—Henry W. Beecher

Angel Shadows

A couple of weeks before Christmas in 1998 , I was
very excited as I opened my new shop—*Angel
Shadows*. The shop was soon busy with people coming to buy
angels and candles of every size. Winter turned to spring and
my gardens were all being revamped. One of the new addi-
tions would be a rather large rock.

I had picked out a verse that I wanted carved on the rock
from a calendar which my girlfriend had given me. On this
calendar was 365 days of wonderful, inspirational sayings as

well as the most beautiful pictures of angels that I had ever seen. The verse for my rock would read;

FROM THE MOMENT OF BIRTH
BEYOND THE LIMITS OF LIFE,
ANGELS WATCH OVER US

Spring came early and so did my wonderful angel rock. I planted beautiful "Angel Face" roses all around it and made a client patio so that everyone could enjoy my garden. Life was going great for awhile, but that was soon to change.

My father had been battling what the doctors felt was pneumonia. I called and could tell right away by his breathing that something was terribly wrong. I called my sister and told her we should take Dad to the hospital.

My father was admitted immediately and although they could see some spots on his lung, it would take many tests to finally conclude that he had a form of lung cancer. A month later we learned at his bedside that it was terminal.

The first amazing thing happened as my sister talked to my father. Very calmly he said something; "I've had 70 great years, but I am only a small piece in a very big puzzle—I would like to go home now". There was no anger in his voice, and no questions. He had come to terms with his own mortality much sooner than we had. So two days later, with oxygen in tow, I picked my father up and took him home. We video taped our last Father's Day two weeks later.

The following weekend, I moved back home to help my mother as her coping skills were ebbing. It turned out, that I wouldn't be staying long. The very next morning, my father said, "I've run out of steam." My father would be readmitted for the last time to the hospital. He became very quiet those last days as he was trying to detach from the family. He was thrilled when my mother and my husband made his funeral arrangements.

I stayed with Dad while they carried out his list of wishes and when they returned, he smiled as they gave him all the details. I had called my brother earlier in the morning and told him that if he wanted to see his father alive one more time, he had better start driving. He was a two day drive from where we were.

My father's health seemed to be failing fast. He was coughing more and eating less. He had been moved to a private room and even the sound of background music was more than he could stand. He was concentrating so hard on staying alive. My brother arrived at 5:45 p.m. He was shocked to see just how frail my father had gotten in the past month. My mother gave my father a cup of tea and then, at approximately 7:15 p.m., my father started to take his oxygen off. My mother kept putting it back on, but I knew that he did not wish to live any longer. I said to my father "You don't want to wear your oxygen, do you Dad?" and he replied "No".

We stroked his head and sang to him and his eyes seemed to focus on things we couldn't see. He started to speak again telling us that he could hear birds. He was in a boat, and the sun was shining. At one point he wanted to climb out of it, and with amazing strength moved to get out of bed. He said he could see the light, and when my sister said "walk toward it Dad", my father took his last breath in this life.

I had asked my angels to make his passing peaceful. And his passing had been without a doubt, peaceful and surreal.

—Linda Cooper

And he lay down and slept under a juniper-tree;
and, behold, an angel touched him, and said
unto him, Arise...
—1 Kings 19:5

Prayer moves the

hand which

moves the world.

—J. A. Wallace

Deer Angel

❧

$\mathcal{J}$ was online at the library, responding to e-mails and prayer requests. As I was praying, I ran across a prayer need from someone who was having severe problems with finances and cars. These areas were my specialty as I had been through three cars in less than a year, so I spent some extra time with this person. I comforted them, and told them from experience that in God's time, it would all work out.

Realizing I had to leave for dinner, I signed off, got my coat and headed out the door. The sun was going down and it was beginning to flurry so I hurried to my car and started the 20 minute ride home.

Driving along, I began thanking God over and over again for my car. Having reliable transportation is something many take for granted, but like all things, not having makes you appreciate the having. I felt lighthearted and thankful.

About six miles out of town, I saw a brown blur to my left. I was doing about 50 miles per hour, and with the lights in front and in back against the white snow it took a moment for my eyes to lock in on it.

A large deer was running toward me.

I hit the brakes, but I knew that hitting it was inevitable. Feet became inches as I slid toward her. I braced for impact hoping that nobody would get hurt in the pile up that was likely to happen next.

Then, as the cars slid to a stop, something came between us, shoving the deer backward into the air, causing it to fly back into the clearing that she came from. The big doe landed in the snow, got up, shook it off, and slowly walked away unharmed.

It took a moment for me to snap out of it. I saw the eyes of other drivers, equally shocked, and realized by their expressions, that we had all seen the same thing.

I replayed it in my mind over and over and began to smile. It was a continuation of the gratitude that I expressed just moments before and I told God again that I love Him.

I don't know how many angels can gather on the head of a pin, but I do know they can slip in between cars with just inches to spare.

—Anonymous

SOME THINGS

HAVE TO BE

BELIEVED

TO BE SEEN.

—RALPH HODGSON

The Messenger

In December of '96 my husband, son and I had just been Christmas shopping Palm Desert. We were on our way home, but I was deep in thought.

Nine months earlier, my 15-month-old daughter had died. I had been going through post traumatic stress syndrome, and major depression. I also spent countless hours, wondering if she was in heaven. I believed in God, and believed she was with Him, but I kept asking God for a sign.

Lots of little things happened that I took as signs, and I was comforted, but continued to ask God for assurance that all was well with my little girl.

To get to our place in Morongo Valley, you must drive this section of road that is long and winding. It was late, and my husband was driving when an angel appeared, right over the windshield of our car. It hung there for what seemed like forever and as I looked up on it, I had an overwhelming feeling of peace. Then, it disappeared.

I sat there silent. I didn't want to say anything. *What if nobody else saw it?*

The quiet was broken by my son.

"Mom and Dad... did you see that angel?"

My husband looked at me and said, "Babe did you see it?"

"Yes." I replied, thankful that all of us saw it.

It had beautiful wings, and where the face and hands were, there was a beautiful light like I have never seen before.

Once we could stop, we pulled over and prayed, thanking God for letting us see this angel.

I have heard that the word *angel* means *messenger*. To me, the appearance of this angel was to give me the message that my sweet daughter Ciara, was indeed in heaven, with God.

It's not every day you see an angel. I wish everyone could. I am telling this story to let everyone know that they can believe in angels and most importantly in God.

—Emily Gonzales

That their hearts might be comforted, being knit together in love, and unto all riches of the full assurance of understanding...
—Colossians 2:2

A Tip from an Angel

This story takes place in 1992, during one of the most memorable Christmas Eves I've ever had. We were very poor and saddened by the fact that we would not be able to buy anything for our little boy. My husband worked off and on but we were in a small town and he didn't get much regular work at this time of year. I worked as a waitress in a corner coffee shop.

I loved the work and I adored the customers. Being a small town, I knew most of them by first name. Christmas was only a week away and I could expect a little extra money from those favorite few customers. I knew we'd have dinner, but really didn't expect anything under the tree.

On the night before Christmas, an elderly man with the sweetest smile came to the window. He had been watching me mop up the floor. I knew he had to be cold out there at that time of night so I smiled back at him and dashed over to the door. He came in and said, "Thank you for being so prompt, it's cold out there."

Before I knew it, we were chatting away, sipping hot cocoa and exchanging stories of Christmas' past. I was finding myself telling him about my family, my little boy at home and how my husband couldn't find work right now but was at home watching our baby. I normally get along well with people, but I found it especially easy to talk to him, and he seemed to know everything I was explaining to him.

Finally, the old man said he needed to get on his way, he had others to tend to that evening. I thanked him for his company and told him that I hoped to see him again. He assured me I would. He offered to pay for his cocoa but I told him it was on me.

He smiled and said, "Well... I'd like to at least leave a tip."

I blushed and said thanks as he opened my hand and pressed a bill into my palm.

Then the door opened and my boss came in. I jumped up and started to explain that I was going to pay for the two cocoas that we had shared. It was a slow night and I didn't figure he'd mind if I sat down for awhile with a customer.

My boss looked around and asked me "What customer? Who are you talking about?"

I looked back where the old man had been sitting and there was not a trace of him. He was just *gone*. There was no way he could have left without my boss and I not seeing him. My eyes teared up as I remembered the tip in my hand.

When I looked inside, I expected to see a dollar, maybe a five. To my complete joy and glee, there was a one-hundred dollar bill. It would be a wonderful Christmas after all.

I know the old man in the coffee shop that day was an angel, sent to me to bless our family and to remind me to always do a good job and be happy I have a job.

—Jeanette Toliver

"For I know the plans I have for you,"
saith the Lord,
"plans to give you a hope, and a future."
—Jeremiah 29:11

GOD LOVES US THE

WAY WE ARE

BUT HE LOVES US

TOO MUCH

TO LEAVE US THAT WAY.

—LEIGHTON FORD

The Little Girl with a Toothless Grin

꧃

Sometimes, ordinary people give angels the day off, and help them in their work. I got a chance to witness an earth angel of sorts one day when I was doing some last-minute Christmas shopping in a toy store.

I was looking for some dolls to buy for my nieces when a nicely-dressed little girl came up next to me with a roll of money clamped tightly in her little hand. When she came upon a doll she liked, she would turn and ask her father if she had enough money to buy it. He usually said "yes," to which she would put it down, find another, and ask again. "do I have enough?"

As she was looking, a little boy wandered in across the aisle and started sorting through some other toys.

He was dressed neatly, but in clothes that were obviously rather worn, wearing a jacket that was probably a couple of sizes too small. He, too, had money in his hand, but it looked to be no more than five dollars or so. He was with his father as well, and kept picking up the toys, but in contrast to the little girl, each time he picked one up and looked at his father, his father shook his head, "no."

Meanwhile, the little girl had apparently chosen her doll. It was glamorous, and in a beautiful dress that would have been the envy of every little girl on the block. However, she had stopped and was watching the interchange between the little boy and his father. Rather dejectedly, the boy had given up on the toy he wanted and settled on a sticker book instead.

As he and his father started walking through another aisle of the store, the little girl put her doll back on the shelf, and ran over to the toy the boy wanted. Her father had a confused look but nodded that she could have it. After speaking quietly with his ear, she raced toward the check-out. I picked up my purchases and got in line behind them.

Then, much to the little girl's obvious delight, the little boy and his father got in line behind me. After the toy was paid for and bagged, the little girl handed it back to the cashier and whispered something in her ear. The cashier smiled and put the package under the counter.

I paid for my purchases and was rearranging things in my purse when the little boy came up to the cashier. The cashier rang up his purchases and then said, "Congratulations, you are my hundredth customer today, and you win a prize!"

With that, she handed the little boy the toy he had wanted all along. He could only stare in disbelief.

"This is what I wanted!" he said enthusiastically.

The little girl and her father had been standing at the doorway during all of this, and I saw the biggest, prettiest, toothless grin on that little girl that I have ever seen in my life. Then they walked out the door, and I followed, close behind them.

As I walked back to my car, in amazement over what I had just witnessed, I heard the father ask his daughter why she had done that. I'll never forget what she said to him.

"Daddy, didn't Nana and PawPaw want me to buy something that would make me happy?"

He said, "Of course they did, honey."

To which the little girl replied, "Well, I just did!" With that, she giggled and started skipping toward their car. Apparently, she had decided on the answer to her own question of, "do I have enough?"

I feel very privileged to have witnessed the true spirit of Christmas in that toy store, in the form of a little girl who understands more about the reason for the season than most adults I know!

May God bless her and her parents, just as she blessed that little boy, and me, that day!

—Sharon Palmer

In all this I have given you an example that by such work we must support the weak, remembering the words of the Lord Jesus, for he himself said, "It is more blessed to give than to receive."

Acts 20:35

If God sends us on

stoney paths,

he provides

strong shoes.

—Corrie ten Boom

The Accidental Angel

*I*f you believe that angels act in unseen ways, directing us in ways that cause blessings to happen to others, then this story is for you.

I bought a house and moved in the first weekend of July. Since I have been in my new neighborhood, I have had the pleasure of meeting a few of my neighbors who seem to be extremely nice people. For Christmas that year, I thought I would do something nice for each of the neighbors that I know. There were nine neighbors whom I knew by name or spoke with often.

I decided to add one more person to my list for a total of ten. The lady I chose lives down the street from me. I see her every morning walking to work as I drive down the street. She always manages a contagious smile and a hearty wave. I had no idea what her name was and wasn't even sure which house she lived in, but thought her friendly nature deserved a gift too.

My idea was to make small fruit baskets and leave them on each of my neighbor's front porches or door steps the night of Christmas Eve. I signed the cards: "Happy Holidays from 2104 Norland Road."

I saved the friendly lady for last, since I was still not exactly sure where she lived. I finally decided upon a house about where I saw her each morning and felt relatively sure that it was hers.

My neighbors really appreciated the baskets. Some called and a couple even came by to thank me.

On my way to work a few days later, I placed my mail in the mailbox and noticed a small note inside. It was addressed simply—Resident, 2104 Norland Road.

I opened the envelope and took out a "Thank You" card. It said; "Thank you for the lovely fruit basket you left on the porch of Richard Kenny. It was very thoughtful. Richard Kenny passed away on January 19, 1999. He never stopped talking about how nice it was that someone remembered him in his time of illness. He really appreciated it."

I was sincerely stunned. I had no idea who Richard Kenny was or that he had been gravely ill. I had left that nice lady's basket on Mr. Kenny's porch by accident. I wanted to say by mistake, but that would be wrong. I believe that Richard Kenny was meant to have that basket and the Lord knew that he only had less than a month to live. It was too bad that the nice lady did not get to receive a fruit basket from me this Christmas, but I believe that if she knew what happened, she wouldn't have had it any other way.

I feel blessed to have helped Richard Kenny's last days be more cheerful. This just further reinforces my belief that there are never any mistakes in life—just detours, shortcuts, and small excursions along the way.

—Aaron Brian Fielder

Take, I pray thee, my gift that is brought to thee;
because God hath dealt graciously with me,
and because I have enough.

Genesis 33:11

Most men forget

God all day and

ask Him at night

to remember them.

—Anonymous

The Mountain Pass

❧

My husband and I were on our honeymoon and were driving from Colorado to California. Our car had broken down so we had gotten a late start going through the mountain passes and to make matters worse, it started to snow.

The snow was coming down so hard all we could see was white and you could barely see the road. My husband was driving way too fast and I just new he was going to end up killing us so I began quietly praying for God to protect us.

Then a miracle happened. As I was saying my silent prayer a glowing figure appeared in front of the car. It matched our speed of 50 miles per hour, staying just ahead of us as we traveled down the road. He glowed brilliantly through the snow like an electric light bulb. I could even see his features and his hair which was long, he wore a long robe and most impressive of all was his size, he was huge.

I assumed I was seeing things until my husband said "Do you see what I see?"

"I don't know" I said, "what do you see?"

He then described the angel.

I said "Yep that's what I see alright"

Thinking maybe we were getting ready to die or something, my husband asked "Is he coming to get us?"

"I don't know." I replied, not knowing what to think.

Just then, we heard the whistle of a train. My husband said, "Oh God where are the tracks!"

He started to brake.

We began to slide through the snow, finally coming to a stop just in time to see the cars of the train flashing by only five feet from the hood of our car.

"Do I believe in angels? You bet!"

—Anonymous

Fear not, only believe.
Mark 5:36

REACH UP AS FAR

AS YOU CAN, AND

GOD WILL REACH

DOWN THE REST

OF THE WAY.

—BISHOP VINCENT

The Milk Man

ꙮ

Most people want presents for Christmas but for many, just having food and the most basic necessities would be the greatest gift of all.

I had been to a Wednesday night Bible Study where the Pastor shared about listening for God with an obedient heart and I couldn't help but wonder, "Does God still speak to people?" I had been a Christian for many years and had heard of people getting "a word from the Lord" but personally, had never heard so as much as a peep.

After the service some friends and I went out for coffee and pie to discuss the subject further. Several talked about how God had led them in different ways and how listening with your ears is not as important as listening with your heart.

At about ten o'clock, we all headed home, and as I drove I began to pray, "God... if you still speak to people, speak to me. I will listen. I will do my best to obey."

Driving through main street, I had the strangest, over-whelming urge to stop and buy a gallon of milk. I couldn't shake it. I looked up and said out loud, "God is that you?" Hearing nothing, and not seeing anything that could pass for a sign, I kept driving.

Still, I couldn't get that gallon of milk out of my mind.

Then I thought about Samuel and how he didn't recognize the voice of God.

"Okay, God, in case that is you, I will buy the milk."

It didn't seem like too hard a test of obedience. I could always use the milk, so I stopped, purchased the gallon of milk, and started off toward home again.

As I passed 7th Street, I began to feel that same overwhelming urge—this time to make a right turn. It was like a powerful magnet pulling at my soul, and I knew that I wouldn't have peace unless I did it.

"This is crazy" I thought. Half jokingly, and glad I was alone in the car, I gave in and said out loud, "Okay, God, I will".

I drove several blocks, when suddenly, I felt like I should stop. I pulled over to the curb and looked around. I was in a semi-commercial area of town. It wasn't the best but it wasn't the worst of neighborhoods either. The businesses were closed and most of the houses looked dark like the people were already in bed. Again, I sensed something,

"Go and give the milk to the people in the house across the street."

I looked at the house. It was dark and it looked like the people were either gone or they were already asleep. I started to open the door and then sat back in the car seat. "Lord, this is insane. Those people are asleep and if I wake them up, they are going to be mad and I will look stupid."

Still, no audible answer from God. There was a turbulence in my soul that could only be answered with faith. Again, I felt like I should go and give the milk.

"Okay God, if this is you, I will go to the door and I will give them the milk. If you want me to look like a crazy person, okay. I want to be obedient."

I walked across the street and rang the bell. I could hear some noise inside and a man's voice yell out, "Who is it? What do you want?"

About then I felt like just leaving the milk and running for the car, but before I could make my move, the door opened.

The man standing there was in jeans and a t-shirt. He looked mussed up like he had just gotten out of bed.

He had a strange look on his face and he didn't seem too happy to have some stranger standing on his doorstep. "What is it?"

I thrust out the gallon of milk, "Here, I brought this for you."

The man took the milk and rushed down a hallway speaking loudly in Spanish. Then from down the hall, a woman came carrying the milk toward the kitchen. The man was following just behind her holding a baby. The baby was crying.

The man began crying, "We were just praying. We had some big bills this month and we ran out of money. We didn't have any milk for our baby. I was just praying and asking God to show me how to get some milk."

His wife yelled out from the kitchen, "I asked God to send an angel. Are you an angel?"

I reached into my wallet and pulled out all the money I had and put in the man's hand. Turning, I walked back toward the car, got in and cried, knowing full well that not only does God hear our prayers, but he uses those who will listen to help answer them.

—Anonymous

Trust in the LORD, and do good; so shalt thou dwell in the land, and verily thou shalt be fed.

Psalm 37:3

WHO DOES THE BEST

HIS CIRCUMSTANCES

ALLOWS, DOES WELL,

ACTS NOBLY; ANGELS

COULD DO NO MORE.

—EDWARD YOUNG

Pray for an Angel

About twenty years ago when my daughter Lori was 19, she decided to drive us to church one Sunday in her "new to her" car. Of course, since her car was just newly purchased, she was not familiar with it and about halfway through our forty-minute drive, the car stopped on a lonely stretch of road.

We had no idea of what might have been wrong. We wondered if the gas gauge was broken and it was just out of gas. I told everyone that we should praise the Lord in all things. It wasn't snowing at least, so my suggestion was to thank God for that much and walk back home.

My daughter was very disappointed and near tears, and said that she was not going to walk home, it would take at least an hour.

"OK, I will pray for an angel!" I said.

The general response was, *yeah, right*.

After ten minutes an elderly woman drove by and stopped. She said that she would be glad to drive us home. We all praised the Lord, thankful that God answered my prayer so quickly.

She was a very likeable woman and we soon were engaged in an animated conversation. I mentioned that we had prayed for an angel while we were stuck.

She laughed and told us that she was a music teacher and had just driven one of her students home. She went on to say that she was never out this way—*ever*.

As she dropped us off at our house she said, "Be specific next time when you pray for an angel, my name in German is ANGEL. I would hate to be across town and have the Lord send me out here again."

—*Rev. Carolyn Madden*

Behold, I send an Angel before thee, to keep thee in the way, and to bring thee into the place which I have prepared.
Exodus 23:20

M~~USIC~~ IS WELL SAID

TO BE THE SPEECH OF

THE ANGELS.

—T~~HOMAS~~ C~~ARLYLE~~

Snowbound Angel

Several years ago. I was driving through the mountains just outside of Steamboat Springs, Colorado. I had finished a week long job in southern Wyoming and wanted to go skiing. Despite snow storm warnings I headed through the mountain pass.

A storm did come, and it was a bad one. I quickly found myself in blizzard conditions. I couldn't even see to the edge of the road and finally, it was snowing so badly I had to stop.

I was terrified and knew that I was in trouble. I can remember praying for God to help me.

Then, a truck pulled up behind me. A man got out and told me to follow him. Still shaking, I followed him for a couple of miles through winding roads. He began to pick up speed though, making it difficult to follow. I couldn't see how he could stay on the road and quickly lost sight of him.

I was still able to make out his tire tracks however, so I followed them to safety to the other side of the storm. Finally, able to see down the road again, I saw that the truck had vanished.

I now believe this guy was an angel sent to help me. If I couldn't see the edge of the road, how could he? There is no way anyone of this world could have navigated that road in those conditions at such a speed.

—Bill Komendant

Have courage for the great sorrows of life, and patience for the small ones. And when you have finished your daily tasks, go to sleep and have peace knowing that God is awake.
—Victor Hugo

Happy Tears

❧

Christmas was never so special as the winter of 1968. That was the year I understood that mommies cry even when they're happy. We were so poor financially, but in our hearts we were the richest family in town.

Mom and Dad tried to give us everything we needed but there were times we didn't have much on the table. My little brother and sister would come to me and ask me for special things and I would have to shush them and keep them from asking too loud as to keep Mom and Dad from hearing. It used to hurt to watch Mom cry because we didn't get the things we wanted all the time. I could tell that it nearly killed Dad to see us go without.

That Christmas was one that I will never forget. We had a little tree that stood tall and lean with a few handmade ornaments on it. We sat down and ate a wonderful supper. Mom always made it with a warm smile and such love in her heart. There were cookies and milk for dessert.

Then Dad began reading to us from the Bible. We heard the story of Christmas and my little brother led us in prayer;

"Dear God, thank you for sending us a baby in a manger and for sending us an angel."

Mom started to cry at the sweetness of what my little brother had prayed. We all smiled and began to sing carols. Laughter and joy filled the room as we sang but we were interrupted by a knocking at the door. Dad got up to answer it and Mom had a surprised look on her face as we had not expected anyone on Christmas Eve. When Dad had turned around to face us he had a box in his hands. Mom asked who it was from and he said he didn't know, there had been no one standing outside at the doorstep, only the box.

Mom said, "open it! open it!" And when she looked inside, she started crying. There were presents inside, plenty for us all, fruit and nuts and candy and cakes. My little brother looked up at Mom and asked why she was crying.

"An angel brought us presents," Mom smiled and said, "Sometimes mommies cry when they are happy, too."

—Diane Lane

Blessed are they that mourn:
for they shall be comforted.

Matthew 5:4

CHRISTMAS BEGAN IN

THE HEART OF GOD.

IT IS COMPLETE ONLY

WHEN IT REACHES

THE HEART OF MAN.

—ANONYMOUS

Foodtown Angel

I lost my job. Business had been slow where I worked, and the possibility of a layoff became a reality a few weeks before Christmas. I rode home with my last check in my pocket, and no clue about what I was going to do next.

My oldest son Ryan was eight, and we had a new baby. There were bills to pay, and the rent was due. I cashed my check and went to the post office to write money orders. We didn't even have a checking account, let alone a savings account. I felt that if I paid off as many bills as possible, it would buy us time until we received the first check from unemployment.

I sent out 11 money orders leaving us with $23.75 in my pocket. By the time I got home I was distraught. My wife, Ruth, was supportive but I knew she was scared. We had some food but were out of baby formula. Ruth called the doctor hoping we could take the baby off of the formula, but our pediatrician said we couldn't. We were in trouble.

I was off to Foodtown, feeling like a total failure. I was sobbing by the time I parked my car. I started apologizing to God, telling Him how sorry I was for everything and for being such a loser. I seldom talked to Him when things were going good and now I felt like a hypocrite, sitting in the Foodtown parking lot asking Him for help.

Regaining my composure I went into the store and bought bread, formula and peanut butter. As I got in line, someone tapped my shoulder. I turned to see a woman dressed in a business suit. She handed me her card and told me she was an employee of the formula manufacturer, and because she saw me buy a can of their product, she was authorized to send me a free case.

My knees knocked and I could hardly write my name and address. I hurried back to the car praying and crying, "Thank you God, thank you God" over and over. And I give you my word, my solemn oath, that I heard Him—*with my ears*—tell me; "Don't worry—trust Me."

From then on, I realized that God wants us to rest in Him and trust that He is watching out for His children.

—Jay Birch

But it is good for me to draw near to God: I have put my trust in the Lord God, that I may declare all thy works.
Psalm 73:28

THE ONLY MEASURE

OF WHAT YOU

BELIEVE

IS WHAT YOU DO.

—ASHLEY MONTAGU

Ice Angel

❧

When I was five years old, my seven year old sister and I decided we were going to sneak out of the house, and go on an adventure.

We set out as our parents slept, and made our way to the river. We wanted to cross it, but the bridge was a long way from where we were. The river was frozen, and seemed strong enough to hold us, so we began to walk on the ice to the other side.

We came to a stretch where there was open water. I said to my sister, "Now what do we do?"

"Swim," she said.

"But I don't know how to swim!"

"Don't worry, I'll carry you on my back" she replied confidently.

I agreed and just as we were getting ready to jump into the quickly flowing icy water a man appeared from out of nowhere.

It scared us so badly that we immediately went back across the ice and returned home. Our parents never even knew we were gone.

Years later my sister and I were reminiscing about this event as our mother sat there with wide eyes and her mouth open in shock. As we talked about it openly, we realized how close we came to death that cold, winter morning. Had it not been for this man, who we believe now to be an angel, we most certainly would have lost our lives.

I am grateful every day for the man at the river's edge and if he was not an angel he was certainly sent by an angel.

—Barbara Smith

*The Lord will keep watch over your going out
and your coming in, from this time
and for ever.*

Psalm 121:8

FAITH IS NOT

BELIEVING

GOD CAN;

IT'S BELIEVING

GOD WILL.

—LEWIS TIMBERLAKE

My Co-Pilot

If I had any doubt about the existence of angels, it all changed on a cold morning just before Christmas in 1990. I was training to finish a commercial pilot rating at a small airport north of Dallas, Texas. That day's training would be comprised of pattern work focusing on what is termed as, "touch and go's." This is exactly what it says it is. A pilot would stay in the traffic pattern and execute a series of takeoffs and landings with new variables, such as a simulation of a short field takeoff, or landing with an obstacle at either end of the runway.

The traffic pattern was full of planes that day. There were six by my count and everyone was in communication with one another. We, as a group, knew where everyone else was, or so we thought.

Communication is not required for landing at that particular field and that seems to be where my story takes a turn. Everything was going nicely that day. Great precision was possible with the light breezes—it really was a nice day. I had lined up on "final" approach. (This is when you have lined up with the runway and you are descending the last 400-500 feet to the runway.) All that's really left is to land the airplane.

I was in the process of descending and was 300 feet above ground level. Something was bothering me—I had the feeling that something just wasn't right. This was a perfect approach so, I ignored the premonition and pressed on, passing it off for nervous energy.

The feeling got worse and I took a glance at my instructor sitting next to me. He was just staring straight ahead, not a word coming from his lips. *Everything must be okay,* I thought as I began to decend to 250 feet. Then, someone said firmly, "Look down!"

With some hesitation, I looked at my instructor, he didn't say it, he didn't hear it, he was just pleasantly staring straight ahead. I was in the bewildered state of trying to figure out what I had just heard, when the voice loudly said "Look down, NOW!"

I looked over at my flight instructor friend and he was as happy as a clam. It was clear he hadn't heard anything.

I looked at him and said in the calmest voice I could muster, "I've got to see something," and immediately tilted the plane using something called a "slip". A slip lets the plane maintain its flight profile, but you gain a huge amount of visibility below the aircraft.

I couldn't believe my eyes, there was a plane directly below mine and perfectly matching my speed! We were going to crash in seconds as we were quickly using up precious altitude! I poured the coals to the engine and aborted the approach, pulling out of disaster's way. My instructor was shocked, and wondering what was wrong with me.

I leaned the plane over and showed him the plane that had nearly killed us. He asked me how I knew it was there. I shook my head and couldn't find a word to say, knowing he would never believe me. The plane had been directly below us, so I couldn't say I caught a glimpse of it out of the corner of my eye. I thought about saying I heard the engine, but you would never hear it over your own. So, I didn't tell him anything. All I could do was keep smiling and shaking my head. Heck, I didn't believe it yet myself!

The other pilots that had shared the pattern with us talked in length on the ground about it. They only saw the mystery plane as I called for a "missed approach." We investigated further to find this aircraft was flown by a very old gentleman who flew everywhere at 200 feet off the ground and didn't use his radio at all.

Now, flying as a commercial pilot, I think back time and again to a clear day in Texas, one that should have been my last, and feel a great amount of comfort knowing I have someone looking over my shoulder,... my co-pilot.

—Chris Hay

Is not the LORD your God with you? and hath he not given you rest on every side?

1 Chronicles 22:18

OUT OF

DIFFICULTIES

GROW

MIRACLES.

—JEAN DE LA BRUYÈRE

Angels Watching

༄

I was only two the last time I saw anyone in my Dad's family. My parents had some bad problems, so it was decided that it would be best for them to stay out of our lives. I'm 15 now, and my whole life I'd always wondered who they were, what they were like, and did I look like them? Filled with curiosity I had tried to find them a few times, but I never could seem to find anything.

Just before the holidays, my Grandma got a call from my Dad's sister who was only 13 the last time she'd seen me. She wanted to know how we were, and if we would like to meet anyone. I called her and we talked and cried most of the time.

Finally I decided I was going to go meet my family. We drove from Houston up to Oklahoma, and I was scared to death. What was I supposed to say to these strangers that were my family? My Grandma and I pulled up to the house, my sister had decided she wasn't ready to meet anyone yet.

Suddenly I wasn't as nervous anymore, I felt peaceful, like everything was going to be okay. After hugging and crying outside, we all went into the house. I never paid attention to the room we were in or where I sat. I just picked a spot and sat. I was too busy trying to remember who everyone was. We took tons of pictures that day, and it was a few days later that my boyfriend Ben took me to get them developed.

I didn't notice anything unusual about them, they looked like normal pictures to me. I was just sitting on the couch surrounded by family. Ben pointed out something funny to me a few days later though. In every picture I was sitting under a painting of a guardian angel. We don't know if it was the flash bouncing off the painting, but in every one it was shining bright.

I don't know if it means anything to anyone, but to me that was my angel. Sitting above me the whole time, watching over me, making sure I was okay.

—Keli

The Lord keeps watch over the spirit of man...
Proverbs 20:27

THERE IS NOTHING
YOU CAN DO TO
MAKE GOD LOVE YOU
MORE, AND THERE IS
NOTHING YOU CAN
DO TO MAKE GOD
LOVE YOU LESS.
—DAVID BUSBY

Armchair Angel

My grandmother owned an old, overstuffed chair that was brown and green plaid. It looked terrible next to her blue sofa and love seat. Yet, regardless of how many years passed by and however many styles of furniture she went through, she kept that old chair. To say it was ugly was an understatement but we all just got used to seeing it around. What made the whole thing funny though, was that she would never let anyone sit in it.

"Grandma, why can't I sit in that old chair?" I would ask.

"Because dear, my Angel is sitting there".

We would all sit around and giggle. Grandma would just look over into the old chair and smile.

It was Christmas time and we were all planning to meet for a reunion at Grandma's house, on Christmas Eve. Aunts and Uncles, sisters, brothers, cousins, we would all be there. We had been bringing over presents to leave under the tree and it was really starting to pile up. There were so many.

I remember my mother suggesting that we could move the old chair out of the way into another room just this one time. Grandma smiled and replied, "No dear, my angel is sitting there".

Again, giggles and snickers broke out as we thought how silly grandma was being.

Again, grandma looked over into that old chair and grinned.

Two days before Christmas, we had picked grandma up to do some last minute shopping. We returned to see presents scattered all over the lawn, the walkway, the steps, and the porch, leading into the house. The front door was open and we thought whoever did this might still be in the house.

Just then, our next door neighbor walked up and said he had seen someone running from the house, throwing all the presents from a big bag. When we inquired as to why someone would rob the house only to leave everything behind, the neighbor said, "He acted like he had encountered someone and was scared! He ran off, yelling "I'm sorry, I'm sorry!" pale as could be.

We looked at each other, our mouths wide open.

Grandma smiled and said.... "I told you dear, my Angel is sitting there".

—*Kelly Brewster*

Let them be as chaff before the wind:
and let the angel of the LORD chase them.

Psalm 35:5

SOMETIMES GOD

DOESN'T TELL US

HIS PLAN BECAUSE

WE WOULDN'T

BELIEVE IT ANYWAY.

—CARLTON PEARSON

Do You Have an Angel Story?

If you have a story you'd like to share with us, come visit our web site at

www.angelseverywhere.faithweb.com

or you can send a letter to

Snow Angels
Premium Press America
P.O. Box 857
White House, TN 37188

We look forward to hearing your story!

Premium gift books from **PREMIUM PRESS AMERICA** include:

I'LL BE DOGGONE
CATS OUT OF THE BAG

STOCK CAR TRIVIA
STOCK CAR GAMES
STOCK CAR DRIVERS & TRACKS
STOCK CAR LEGENDS

GREAT AMERICAN CIVIL WAR
GREAT AMERICAN COUNTRY MUSIC
GREAT AMERICAN GOLF
GREAT AMERICAN GUIDE TO WINE
SNOBBERY
GREAT AMERICAN OUTDOORS
GREAT AMERICAN STOCK CAR
RACING

ANGELS EVERYWHERE
MIRACLES
SNOW ANGELS

ABSOLUTELY ALABAMA
AMAZING ARKANSAS
FABULOUS FLORIDA
GORGEOUS GEORGIA
SENSATIONAL SOUTH CAROLINA
TERRIFIC TENNESSEE
VINTAGE VIRGINIA
TREMENDOUS TEXAS

TITANIC TRIVIA
BILL DANCES FISHING TIPS
DREAM CATCHERS

PREMIUM PRESS AMERICA routinely updates existing titles and frequently adds new topics to its growing line of premium gift books. Books are distributed though gift and specialty shops, and book-stores nationwide. If, for any reason, books are not available in your area, please contact the local distributor listed above or contact the Publisher direct by calling 1-800-891-7323. To see our complete backlist and current books, you can visit our website at www.premiumpress.com. Thank you.

Great Reading. Premium Gifts.